Toys, painted by W. Trier;

Oskar Seyffert, Walter Trier

TOYS

PAINTED BY W. TRIER

DESCRIBED BY

O. SEYFFERT

PUBLISHED BY ERNST WASMUTH A.G.

BERLIN

Children when at play are really creating artistically Kind fate has endowed us with a beauteous gift to accompany us through life And this gift is art. The miraculous flower does not always blossom as we would have it do Many things, above all a wrong education, often cause it to wither or spoil and die And then we are the poorer for having lost a divine possession.

A little girl will build a Garden of Eden out of some sand and pebbles and blades of grass She puts gaudy flowers in it and is happy in her play. Yes, she is much richer than we are. She creates a paradise out of trifles, a paradise which we can never succeed in creating with all our superior wisdom. And then her mother comes.

She does not see the work of art, the paradise, but she thinks that perhaps the child may get dirty. She only sees sand, earth, and pebbles She drags her child away and scolds her. But it is not from the "dirt" alone she tears her, but from the Heaven her little soul was dwelling in.

Harry is sitting at table and drawing. His cheeks are flushed, his eyes sparkling. He is busy with his art His father enters and enquires. "Harry, what are you doing there?" "I'm painting a beautiful town " "You silly boy, you can't do that Stop that nonsense, and draw some straight lines. That is a good deal more sensible. Draw them nice and straight. And when you've done, then you may draw a circle. That's the way I learnt at school "

The father spoils drawing for the boy; just in the same way as many teachers have done in their classes, and still are doing. They stifle the feelings of a little artist with their pedagogical methods. The father robs his child of a joy, and gives him nothing in return, save mere intellectual rubbish, sorry trash thought out by man who squeezes his poor stuff into a framework of scientific rules

The two examples illustrate a piece of life

What we have said of home-life applies in general to school-life There we learnt a lot of knowledge right the way up to the university Much of it was dry-as-dust science. But our feelings and susceptibilities were mostly neglected In fact, they were not only often not considered, but stifled And then science remained lifeless and could not come to life We had forgotten that culture — for we consider ourselves to be cultured, do we not? — does not only consist of knowledge, but also of feelings, that we had become one-sided and pitiable creatures who had closed the gates of Heaven on themselves in spite of all they had learnt. Intellect is not the key to Heaven, nor the means of fathoming it. Here we understand by Heaven art.

Art is feeling.

Art is, *au fond*, religion.

We learnt to know the world through our ears and the outward eye But we have not found out how to see with the inward eye, for we do not understand by seeing the mere registering of objects around us, the mere writing in the book of our brain, briefly, we do

4

not only understand by seeing the function which a camera can execute

Seeing means creating and forming

Only then does seeing come to life

The one-sidedness of our education has been recognized nowadays more than ever And we are casting about for help The future school training combined with handicrafts will help us along new paths Let us hope that enough teachers will be found willing to be apostles of the new thought True, to be a teacher then will mean more than ever to be one of the few Art, and the sense of art must not again be dragged down to the position of a mere unnecessary side-line

Our book is dedicated to children's play. We should be running counter to our idea if we were to treat the subject from a literary point of view Our book is meant to illustrate The pictures, not the words must speak

The toy itself is the main object Its home has been for long centuries in Saxony in the Erz Mountains There toy-making is and was the people's art. The art of the people is imbued with a soul We cannot maintain that this is the case with machine-made productions The toys illustrated in this book came from the Saxon Museum of Folk Art. and are now in the Jaegerhof in Dresden This old building stands like a fairy-castle amid its surroundings, and it has also fairy-tales for our hurried and immature epoch

Toys are strange things. It is not every writer who can tell fairy-tales nor every artist who can design toys I believe but few can I would remind my readers of the toy designing competitions. Specialists sat in judgment on the craftsmen. But in many cases, those for whom the trouble was taken rejected the productions They were the real specialists. the children They did not want the toys that had been recommended to their parents by so many art journals They often threw the much-lauded art productions into a corner and returned to their old familiar playthings

The art of the people has its own secrets.

A natural and strong feeling for form and colour does not preclude a peculiar conventionalizing But there is something natural in conventionalizing Nothing artificial or forced. And just in this the craftsmen have sinned Their products were not naive, but forced. They were too learned in their conception The child, being natural, was enstranged and refused such gifts. And their parents, with their warped ideas, could not understand this attitude

Alas! the soul of the child has been damaged by the fact that the educational value of toys has not been correctly estimated.

Little Anne strokes and kisses her simple dolly a thousand times a day, and loves it dearly Her imagination dresses it to-day in a blue silk dress, and it is a princess. To-morrow it is a poor suffering child that has to be tucked up in its warm cot The day after to-morrow it is a proud rich prince — for there is no limit to imagination. And if the parents of this happy child give her a new doll with real curls, and which can open and close its eyes, and really cry when it is clasped to her heart,

6

and wears an expensive dress . well, then the child no longer needs her imagination; the doll is quite perfect, and there is nothing more to be made of it, no room left for imagination to create and form.

Of course, the time will come when Anne no longer values her first simple doll, and yearns for the second one But the longer she cannot have everything, the richer she remains

A little boy is sitting on chairs turned topsy-turvey, and is puffing, panting, and whistling. He is playing at trains. He himself is the engine. His coloured wooden toy figures are the passengers who get in and out. How much better off he is than his friend who has got a mechanical train which runs "quite alone" round the room. Its owner cannot do much with it, as his part of the game is done when he has wound it up. At last he examines the works, breaks them, and the expensive toy is a dead thing

A Punch and Judy show is a lovely toy to while away the time with My boy invited his friends to see his once a month And they each had to play a piece they had made up themselves. Those were never-to-be-forgotten days And even for us grown-ups there were new revelations. What harmless frolic, fun, and jokes greeted us!

Christmas is the children's festival, and the day for toys But our children are not only to have presents given to them. They must give presents they have made themselves. They must deck the Christmas-tree with decorations they have made themselves: with coloured and golden stars They will then feel the same joy that the dwellers in the Erz Mountains feel, when each year they make anew the toys for the festival of festivals. Weeks before Christmas old and young are all busy making painted figures of the infant Jesus in the manger with the shepherds around it, also candlesticks in the shape of miners, and the multi-coloured "mountain spiders", as the wooden candelabra that are hung up at Christmas are called. And old and young are merry at their work.

It is this merriness we need so sorely

We town-dwellers "buy" our festival. What a difference!

And now enough of examples. Let us look at the pictures Our book is due to the inspiration received from the German "Heimatschutzbund", and will tell of the wealth we possessed, especially in former times, in our toys, and in the wealth that found expression, not in outward pomp, but in the manner of thinking. We have grown poor— may this book be a contribution towards making us richer and better, us, and our children.

O Seyffert.

This is a proud rider from the Seiffner district His horse has very valuable and practial qualities. It has no legs, which after all break off so easily when we play with it Its tail has the advantage that its rider can lean against But, for the rest, the owner is sitting very nobly and with great decorum on a first-class thoroughbred

The girl with the lamb is a fine toy. The shepherdess is really dressed very beautifully, and has on her hat a lovely soft feather which is gently stirred by the wind. But the snowy fleece of the lamb she is driving is much softer, and much more beautiful It is a great pleasure to stroke the lamb. But we should have very clean hands when we do

When the children cannot yet walk properly they are first put in a wooden ring with four legs. There they cannot fall over and hurt themselves, and don't cry, and their mother need not feel afraid about them all day long. It is particularly nice if the owners of such toys can pull them along and seldom fall down themselves Otherwise the toys laugh at them The other toy is a long needle-case Its head can be screwed off. But it is very useful as a doll too

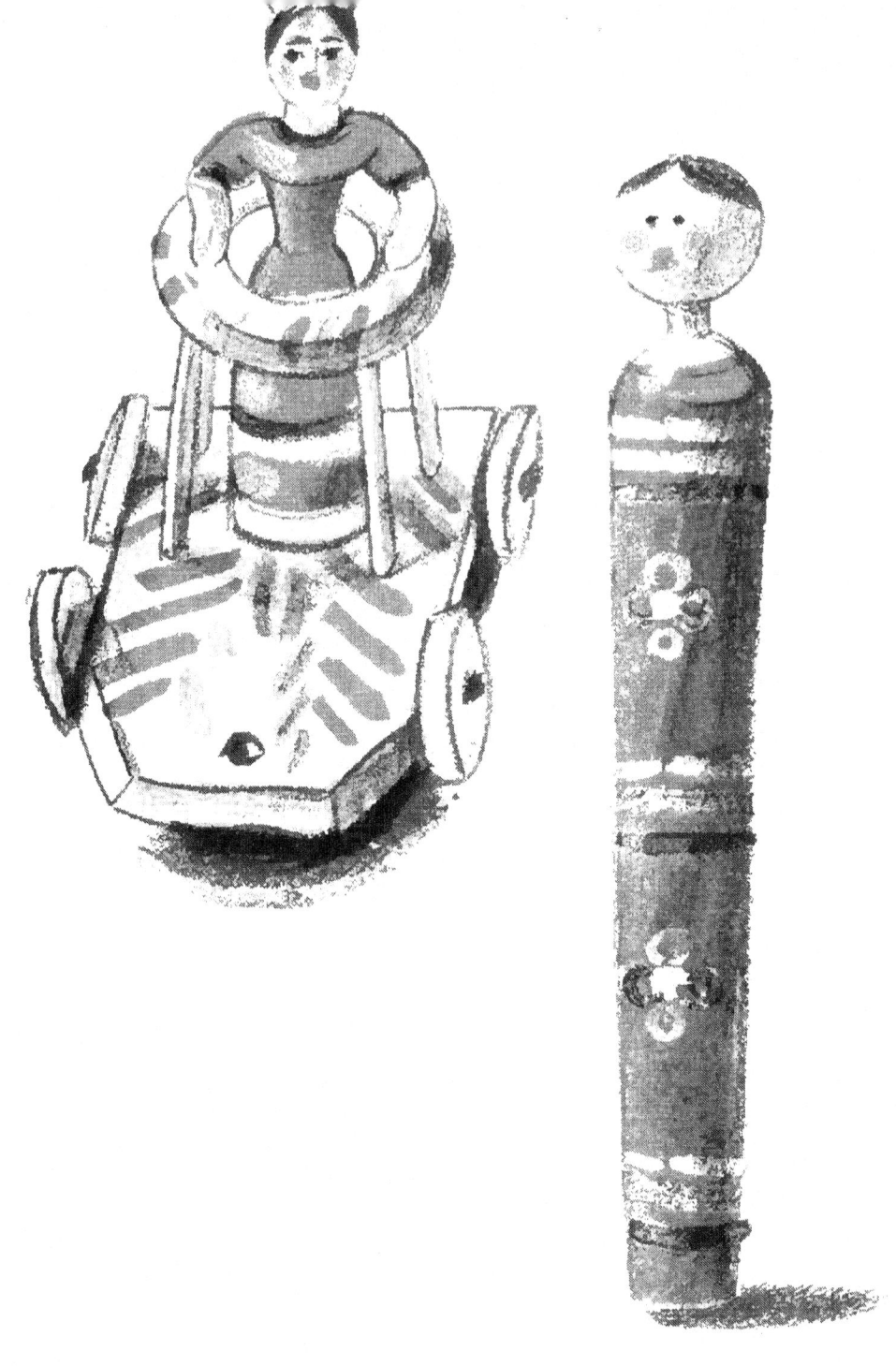

This Christmas angel is larger than you might think from the drawing It is seventeen inches high. A woodman made it for his children He was a good craftsman The angel is holding a red cross in her right hand, and around her head there is a whole wreath of little candles which are all lighted on Christmas Eve And that looks very pretty

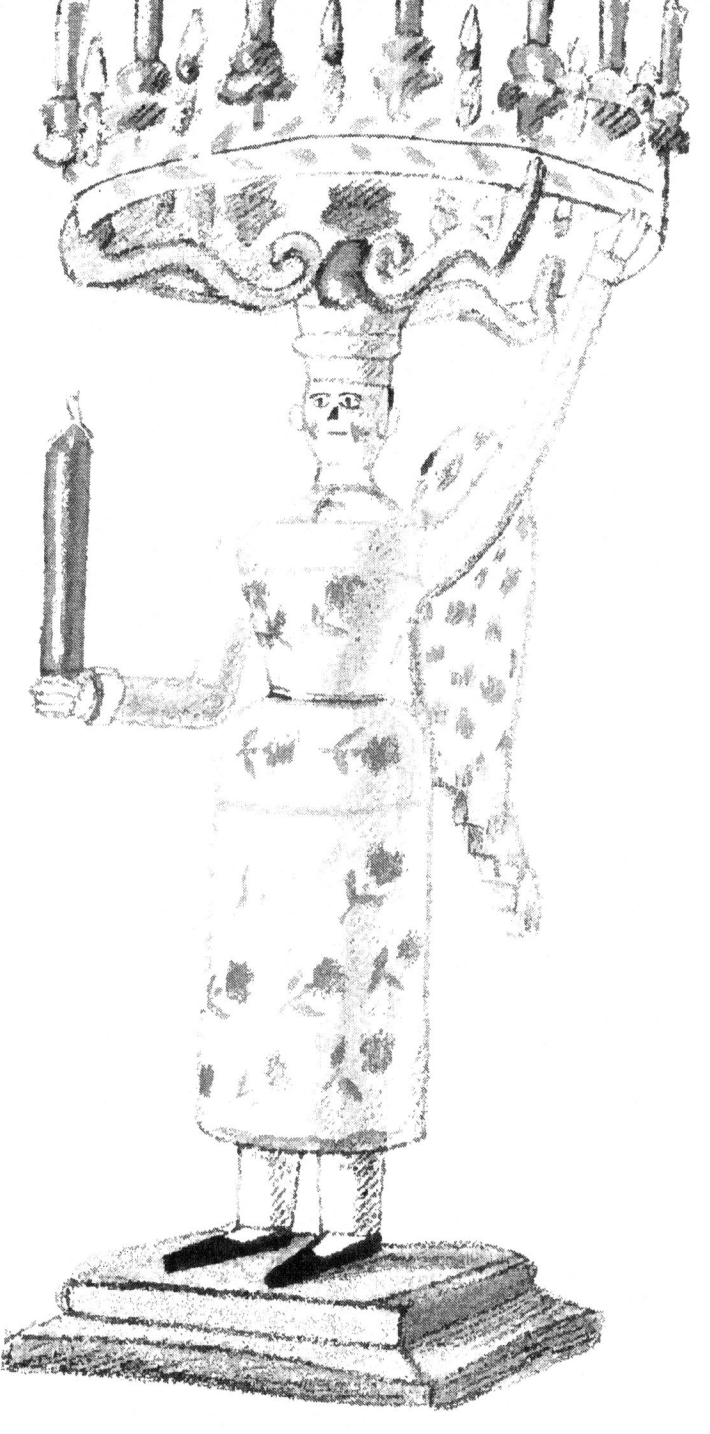

The Jacks-on-strings are a very mixed company They are all dressed up in their best clothes, and they wear particularly fine hats. Some look like soldiers, some like Punch, but they are all in jolly mood If you pull the string they jerk their arms and legs about very quickly, and are quite full of joy They do make you laugh then

Plate 6

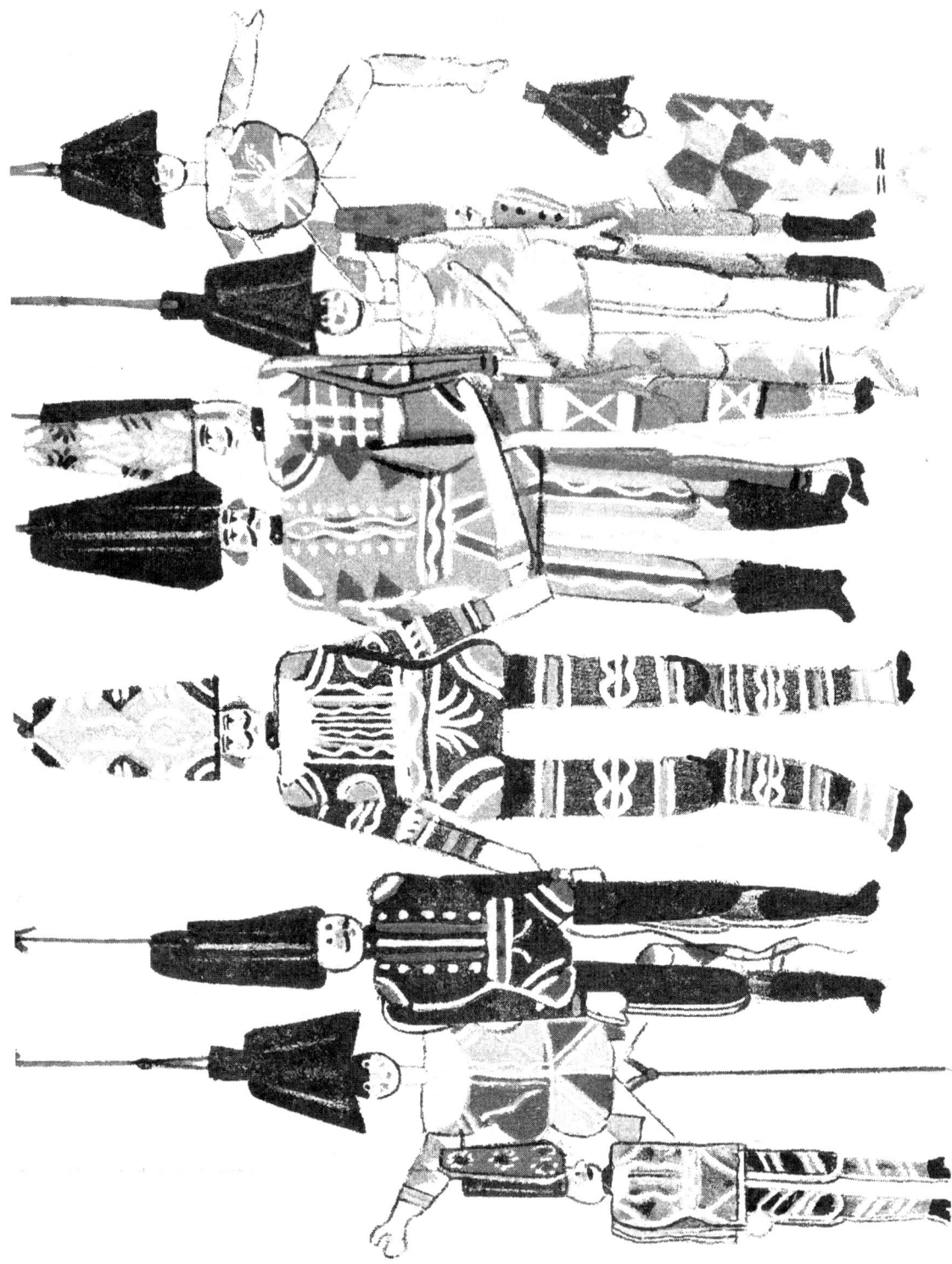

Such Turks stand during Christmas on the wardrobe, on the Christmas-table, and, above all, on the window-sill. They look down into the street, and their candles glitter and reflect a hundred-fold in the shining snow They even have a candle in their turban like the boys who go to matins early in the morning in Neudorf near the Fichtel Mountains, and who have a candle stuck in their golden cardboard crowns. I think such Turks are meant to remind us of the three Magi. But sometimes they remind us of the little figures of men used as fumigators

Plate 7.

Although there is no mining any longer in the Erz Mountains, yet the miner still plays a great part there True, the solemn miners' parade, and the procession to matins are gone, but the pitmen, foremen, and overseers carved in wood are set up at every festival. Our figure is carrying a garland in which lights are fixed like those on a Christmas-tree

Plate 8.

Herr Arthur Ganzauge of Dresden is a fine fellow He makes his own Punch and Judy show and his own figures. And then his wife decks them out in coloured clothes A celebrated painter who has seen all his work maintains that he is an expressionist Herr Ganzauge did not know what to reply to that. Our picture shows us a scene from "Mr Punch in Turkey"

Plate 9

Really, we must repeat that Herr Punch and Judy Ganz-auge knows how to carve his figures. When Death appears, the children are afraid. He is in a white shirt, but not a very clean one, as he comes up out of the dirty ground. The children also fear the robber who looks so horribly at them out of his one eye. But when Punch comes, they laugh and clap their little hands and are very happy, because the brave fellow knocks them about till they are as dead as a door-nail.

Plate 10.

The pig with her six little ones is not really a toy She is a money-box, with which however one can play quite nicely But, as the money-box has to be broken when it is quite full, it is made of clay That is easier to break than wood. It was made by a Dresden potter in 1875; and so it has lasted a long time This is certainly astonishing

This hen is also made of clay. It is very strange that the little chickens are slipping about on her back instead of keeping warm under her wings. This hen is not a money-box, but a sort of whistle. A very amusing toy.

Plate 12.

Mr Nutcracker has a very big head. For this reason he can crack the largest nuts He has a rabbit-skin cap, and his beard is remarkably like rabbit-skin too His clothes are very coloured He comes from Olbernhau

Plate 13

These two are racing. We shall read in the paper that
red won, and blue was a head's length too late

Our rider, who is very tall, is sitting in a somewhat in-
clined attitude on his horse. He is leaning back nearly
too much to be considered a good horseman He and
his steed make a strange ornament But I like them

Plate 15

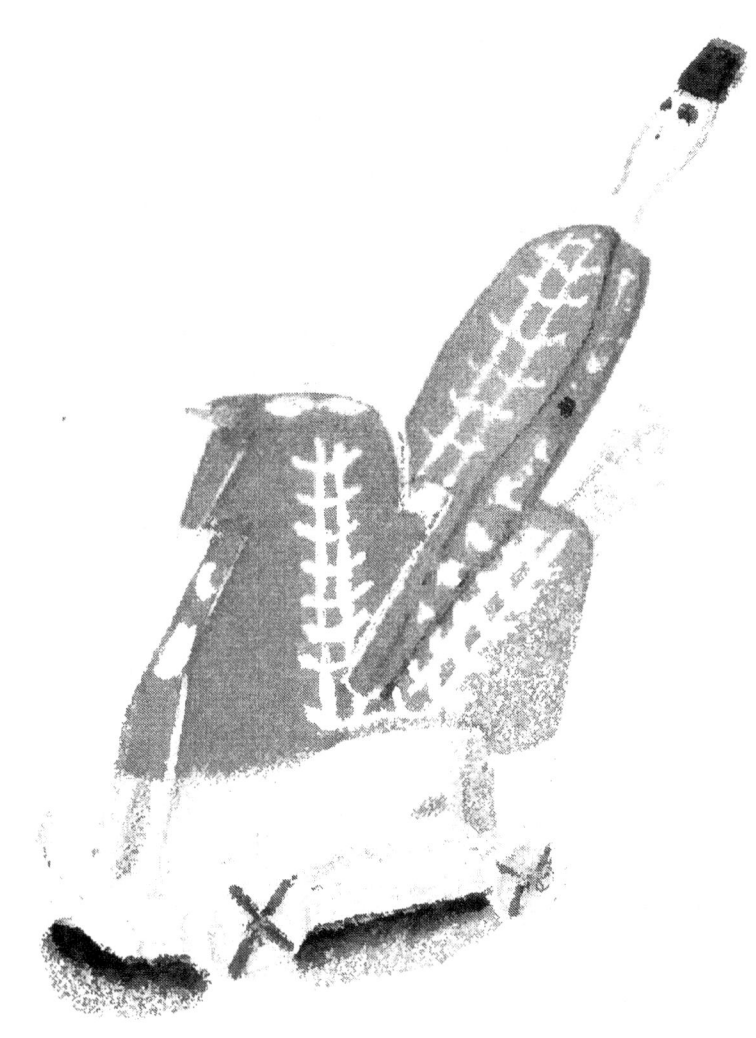

When the air in the room gets worse and worse, Mr Fumigator must come to our aid. We lift up his top part and put a fumigating candle in him. The fumes come out of his open mouth as though the long-bearded rogue were smoking his pipe, and soon the room is filled with pleasant vapours

While the husband is climbing carefully up the ladder to look into the dove-cot and see whether any little ones have crept out of the eggs, his wife is feeding the pigeons with oats so as to make them nice and fat If you turn a handle during this meal, the music plays· "Be true, be true, my love!" At least, that is what it sounds like.

Plate 17

Riding on a merry-go-round to music is one of the greatest pleasures in this world Our merry-go-round has two stories, one on the ground-floor, and one on the first. And you can ride in the latter if you don't get giddy

Plate 18

We are all pleased when at Christmas the "mountain spider", that is the candelabrum, hangs from the ceiling Ours is particularly beautiful On top there is a little temple with Mary and Jesus Below, a train is taking a lot of people to Bethlehem to worship the child The train is crowded

Plate 19

We see a number of wild and tame animals going for a walk in our picture An elephant, a cow, a lion a bear, and two poodles They are already old, and belong to the eighteenth century Or perhaps they come from Noah's Ark We see at once that they are made of wood Former toy-makers could carve and paint much better than those of to-day, but the latter could learn to do so again if they would get this book and look at it carefully

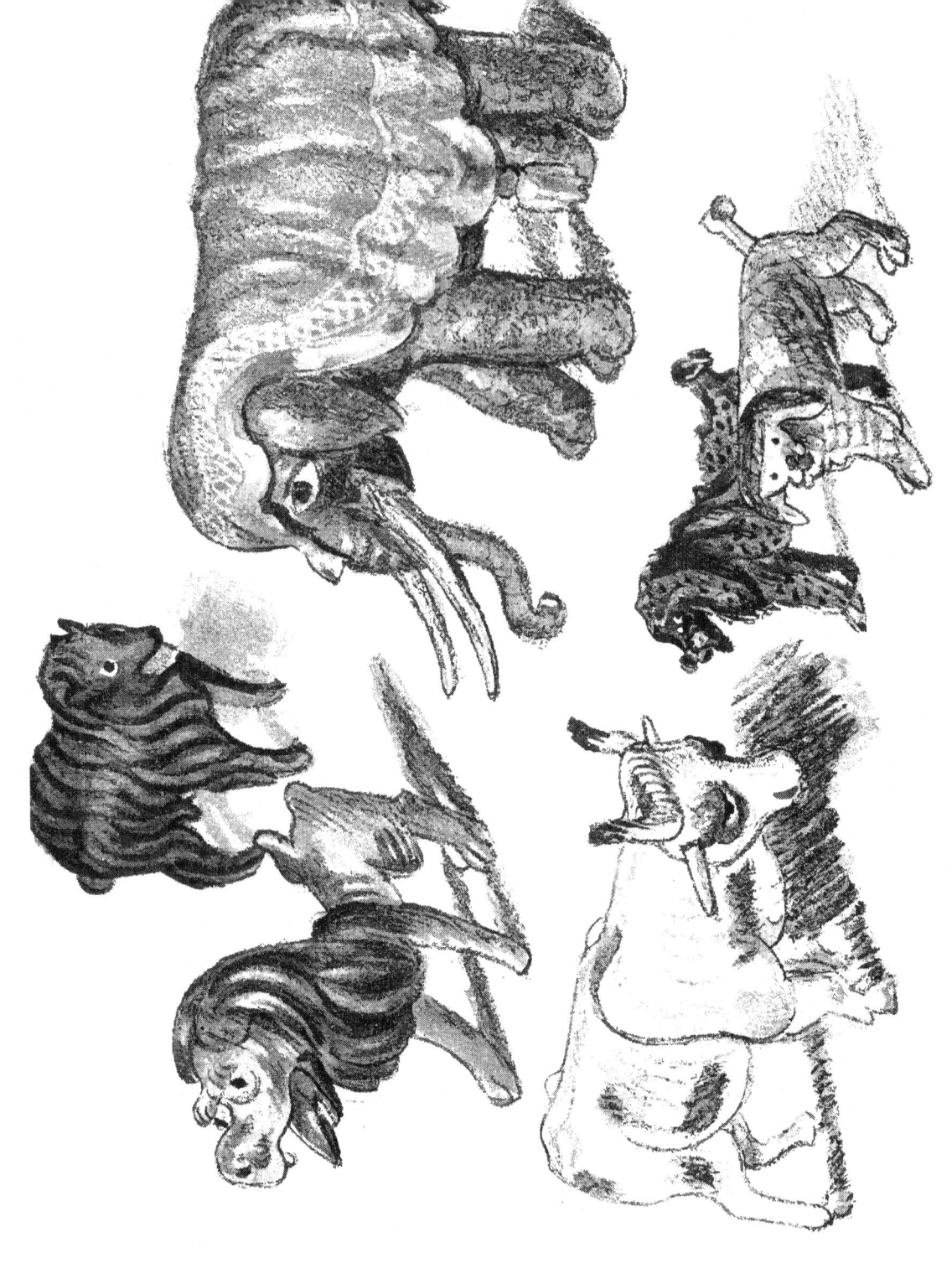

A good hunter hits the stag at the first shot Our hunter
has certainly let his animal come very near Hunter and
stag come from the wooded Heidelberg district

Plate 21.

Here is a shepherd, who, alas! has no legs He is looking
after two sheep He has his house with him, and it runs
on two wheels, so that when it rains, or the wolf comes,
he can go in and sit down If you turn the handle behind,
you will hear a fine and tender melody The sheep like
to listen to it very much.

Plate 22.

Our doll is a toy for big girls It is as large as a little child It is leaning cosily in the corner of the sofa. Its face is shining with pleasure, just the way a peasant girl's face shines after a good wash in cold water before a party

Plate 23

Adam and Eve are standing straight as darts under the apple-tree. The cunning snake is seen leering from under the leaves which half hide it. The group probably decorated a little Garden of Eden under a Christmas-tree. The Christmas-tree is growing in the Garden of Eden. Isn't that beautiful?

Oh! there are pretty ladies with just as pretty servant-maids; tall and slender. They are discussing the news together They are made of paper, and that is why they are so delicately formed Their home is Dresden in Saxony, where beautiful girls "grow"

Plate 25

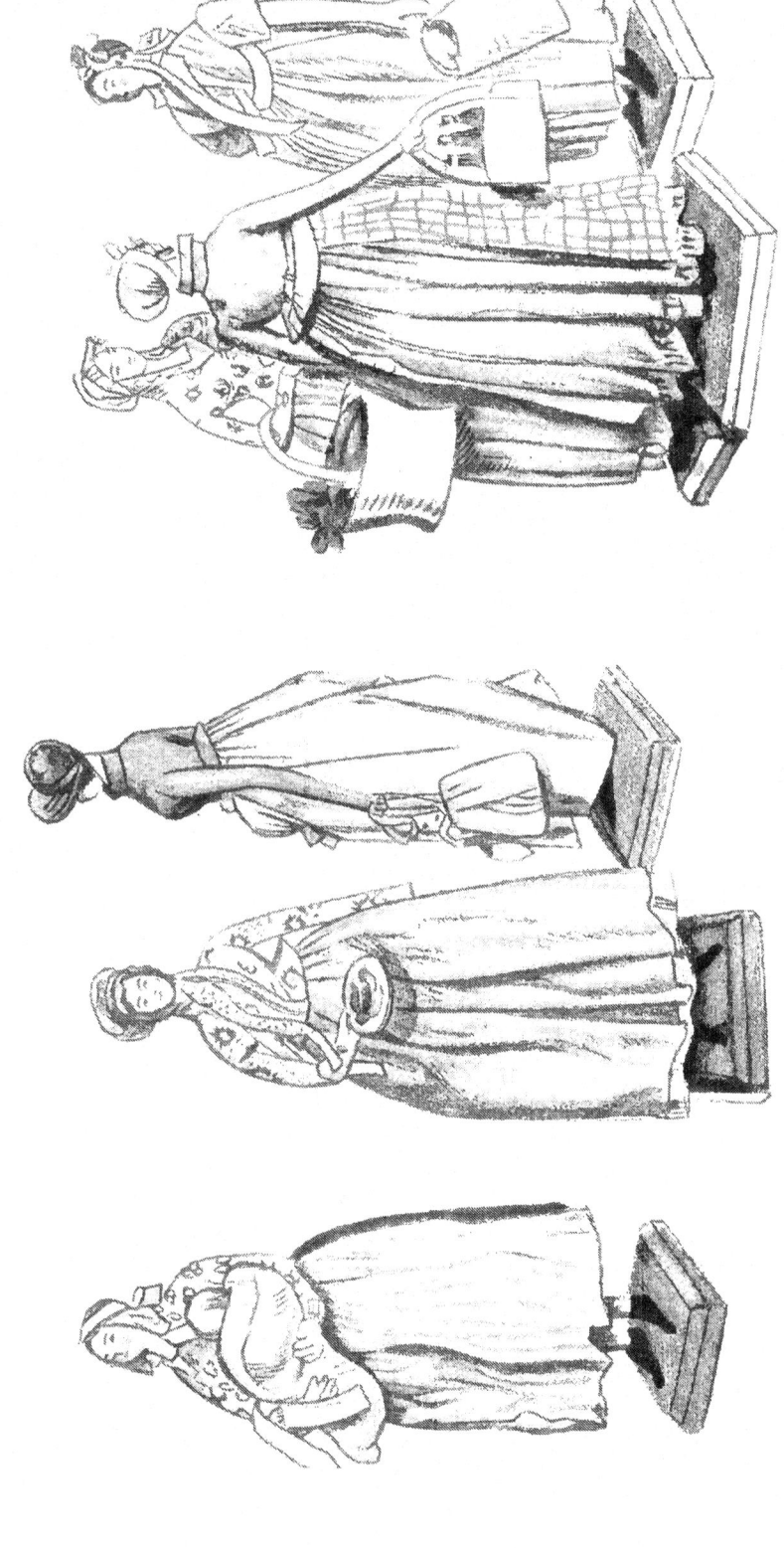

Shooting at a target is a manly sport. Eye and hand are steeled On this Georgian target we see a noble hunter having a quiet nap A little dog is keeping watch over him It is difficult to guess its breed A pretty maid is approaching to bind the dreamer with a chain of roses. Let us hope she will succeed I don't think the dog will bite her

Plate 26

The three Magi from the East are riding day and night on camels led by faithful slaves Sometimes these ships of the desert look a bit strange, as their maker never saw real camels Our group is from Loessnitz where the Carvers' Guild exhibits each year a whole heap of many hundred Christmas-toys People come and look at them, and they need not pay for doing so

Plate 27

Now the tin soldiers appear On top we see an old Saxon grenadier, a captain of horse, and a trumpeter in full-dress uniform Below a captain on a snorting dappled grey followed into battle by a drummer Those who want to see more must go to the Museum of Folk Art in Dresden, where whole battle pieces are set up. It is worth while, and when you are there, you will not want to leave

Plate 28.

Stags and does, and even a wild boar and a fox are fleeing past us followed by mounted huntsmen and greedy dogs. It is not easy to shoot at the timid game with a pistol or gun while mounted Let us hope that the hunters won't hit their leader by mistake. As these figures are fixed on slender wires, they tremble at the least movement as though they were alive

Plate 29

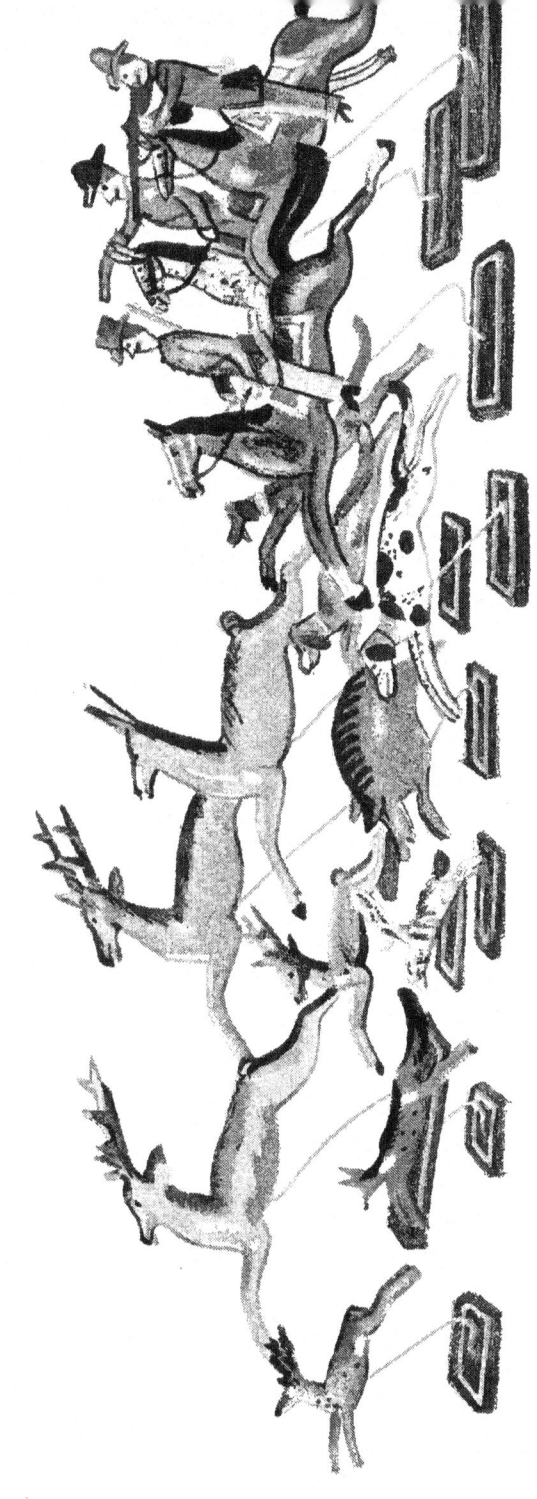

Here we can admire the officers, drummer and soldiers in red coats, white trousers, and busbies They have a long march behind them, for they have come from the Upper Erz Mountains

Plate 30

To play with these sweet little birds affords a lot of variety and pleasure Some of them are made of real feathers, others of wood. Which do you like best? That is difficult to say

Plate 31

Roses, tulips, pinks, and also other flowers grow in a well-kept garden Between them are trees and beds It is pleasant to walk among such splendours The children are in company of grown-ups who keep them out of mischief.

Plate 32

The rider on the fiery black horse was once together with his comrades in a large stable with little Jesus under the Christmas-tree of a wealthy Dresden family. And so we see that warriors also did homage to the child. And the child expressed his great pleasure

.

Plate 33

The dolls we shall now see belong to a collection which little girls would like to have But there are also grown-ups who have the same wish. The first doll is a fine little figure in a white embroidered muslin dress from the period of 1840. She is the oldest.

Plate 34.

These four dolls belong to about the year 1845 It is difficult to tell the age of ladies quite correctly. They are talking about past fashions, and how carefully the owners of dresses used to handle them. If they hadn't they wouldn't have kept so long. Nowadays many children break their toys at once.

Plate 35.

The last one is a doll from 1860. She looks somewhat defiantly about her A more modest behaviour would certainly be more becoming Dolls — as well as children — have various characteristics That is, the dolls of those days. Those of to-day all look nearly alike

Plate 36.

The fair is in the old Margravian town of Meissen where the pretty little tin figures were cast Linen and ribbon sellers, pictures of dreadful deeds, a lithe girl on stilts, a boot booth, a gypsy with a dancing bear, and above all excellent performing dogs make the time fly quickly, and combine the useful with the pleasant

Plate 37

The shy roe standing behind three trees espies a good deal. Lumbermen have come and are felling a slender fir-tree. A man with the local dosser for carrying wood on his back is giving an exact report to the strict head-forester Two women are standing at a respectful distance. In the foreground trunks are being cut and loaded up on to waggons

It must be much more fashionable and pleasant to ride in a state coach and four than in a motor-car There you sit, as I have read in fairy-tales, very comfortably on silk cushions, and look sometimes out on your left side, and sometimes out on your right And if you see any one, you give a friendly nod, and the people greet you respectfully But if you are in a motor-car, the foot-passengers often scold about the dust In fact, some of them even swear, and use very ugly words

These puppets, which are moved by wires from above,— and not, like Punch and Judy figures, from below — were made by a Dresden father in 1845 for his dear children, and once in a while he gave them a performance in a little theatre he had built himself The puppets are not much laiger than those on the picture A gentleman, two good children, and another gentleman are chosen as examples. They are fine toys I don't believe there are any finer. In fact, the whole book is the nicest you can imagine

Plate 40

Lightning Source UK Ltd.
Milton Keynes UK
UKOW05f2324250716

279232UK00010B/427/P

9 781172 299256